Universal Neurasthenia: Or The House Of Rest

Margaret Doane Gardiner

In the interest of creating a more extensive selection of rare historical book reprints, we have chosen to reproduce this title even though it may possibly have occasional imperfections such as missing and blurred pages, missing text, poor pictures, markings, dark backgrounds and other reproduction issues beyond our control. Because this work is culturally important, we have made it available as a part of our commitment to protecting, preserving and promoting the world's literature. Thank you for your understanding.

UNIVERSAL NEURASTHENIA
or The House of Rest

BY
MARGARET DOANE GARDINER

ROBERT GRIER COOKE, Inc.
NEW YORK   MCMVII

Copyright 1907, by
ROBERT GRIER COOKE, INC.
All Rights Reserved

TO MY SISTER
M. S. F.

Universal Neurasthenia

OR

THE HOUSE OF REST

DRAMATIS PERSONAE

Elizabeth (escaped from the German Garden).
Milicent (sprung from the House of Mirth).
Juliette (run away from Bernard Shaw).
Tony (too hard for Harding Davis).
Mark Stone (a wielder of Edged Tools in the Jungle).
Etheldred Ranisty (one of Mrs. Humphrey's Wards—come of age.)
Dr. Wheat-I-Eat (Return to Nature!)

Scene—a garden. Sign on tree,—House of Rest, Dr. Wheat-I-Eat.

(Enter Dr. W., right, carrying letters, a target, pistol, book, basket of stockings, trowel and weed basket. Sets target stage left at back, lays pistol on ground near it, sets basket on steamer chair left centre, front, lays trowel and weed basket right front beside flower bed, muttering.)

Dr. W.—"Plenty of fresh air—nothing like fresh air for exhausted nerves! Don't wonder they are exhausted! Simply worked to death, harping on one string. Great mercy the public got nervous prostration too from reading about them; gives the poor creatures a chance to relax! Whole world forbidden to read novels! Great, great! And these poor overdone types returning to nature! Well, well, it's a great work."

(Enter Elizabeth, left, languidly, caressing a fern.) "Good morning, Miss Elizabeth! Tut-tut, no ferns allowed you know. Put it down!"

Eliz.—"Ah, not to be trampled by the heavy foot of the Man of Wrath!"

Dr. W.—"Man of Wrath! So you've had that nightmare again?"

Eliz.—"Yes, oh yes. I was again the aspiring, gasping wife of the great oppressor. The dream haunts me, and my beloved flowers were no comfort last night. The pansies laughed at me." (Weeps.)

Dr. W.—"Dear me,—a very obstinate case! My dear Miss Elizabeth, you really must not give way so. I think the course of treatment that I have prepared for you this morning will be very bracing to these morbid nerves."

Eliz.—"You hurt me when you call it nerves. I know that those, who tore me from my vegetable affinities and sent me here, called it so; but to me my disease seems but an over-expansion of the soul."

Dr. W.—"Well, well, as you please, my dear, but we must certainly try to *shrink* your soul then. You will take this pistol and aim it at that target. Let it be your ambition to hit the bull's eye."

Eliz.—"You wish me to point *this* thing at *that* thing? What will happen?"

Dr. W.—"Nothing, if you merely take aim, but my idea broadens from that preliminary effort to the more effective actions. You will raise this hammer. Then,—without closing your eyes,—you will pull this trigger towards you."

Eliz.—"Will it make a noise? My spirit abhors an uproar!"

Dr. W.—"The noise will be slight,—the danger nil, as

the pistol will be loaded only with this rubber-tipped arrow, which after hitting the target must be retrieved and placed in the pistol. Excellent, bracing, and absorbing occupation for your morning hours. (Sternly.) You will kindly not distract yourself by noticing natural objects. But for the beneficial effects of fresh air, I should not let you do this in the garden at all. Put your eye on the bull's eye, and keep it there."

Eliz. (her hand to her head)—"Yes, yes, I will endeavor to starve my heart and constrain my soaring soul to this mechanical exercise. But first let me study my weapon. (Enter, right, Milicent.) Ah, Milicent, good morning." (Returns to pistol.)

Dr. W.—"Good day, Miss Milicent."

Mili.—"Four thousand dollars to Mme. Greene, and the quarter's allowance will only be a thousand! O Dr. Wheat-I-Eat, if you would only set up a casino here, a roulette wheel, 'petits chevaux,' something amusing and at the same time useful, I might make enough money that way to pay my debts. I should stop at nothing."

Dr. W.—"Now, my dear young lady, I want to hear no more of debts or gambling. You were sent here to forget the Smart Set."

Mili.—"I cannot!"

Eliz.—"Dear Milicent, you would be so happy if you would let your geologic, botanic soul reach out to the humanity of the stones and plants."

Mili.—"If there were anything to be gained—"

Eliz.—"Peace, joy, content."

Mili.—"How dingy!"

Dr. W.—"I hope you slept well?"

Mili.—"No. When I was Dummy I had to make it spades, no one doubled, and the deal passed on, so I got no sleep."

Dr. W.—"Dear, dear,—the old bridge hallucination! (To Eliz.) Happily there are no cards in the house. (To Mili.) Now, Miss Milicent,

I must ask you to turn your attention to this bed. It is full of weeds, which the gardener has most thoughtfully sowed there for you to dig out. Here is a trowel to help you with the most obstinate ones, but in general they are pulled up with the fingers, so. That will occupy you till lunch."

Eliz. (running across to Dr. W.)—"Oh, let me do it! Dear soil of my heart! Precious weeds!"

Mili.—"*I* cannot consent to do such work."

Dr. W.—"Madame, you are under my orders! Miss Elizabeth, kindly continue your study of that pistol! Miss Milicent, will you remove your gloves? I wish you would dress more suitably!"

Mili.—"Sir, I cannot breathe without gloves, and if for the sake of my health, I condescend to do this menial task, I shall do it *gloved*. As to my clothes,—mere last year's rags,—if I were not dressed as I am, I might be mistaken for a mere human being such as I have been brought up to despise. (takes trowel.) I shall break my back, however, at this game. Kindly get me a chair."

Dr. W.—"I expect you to kneel or squat while you weed."

Mili.—"Kneel! Squat! Well,—the attitude may be effective! I will try it." (Kneels, takes trowel, and delicately pulls up one small weed. Enter Juliette, right.)

Dr. W.—"Ah, Miss Juliette!"

Juliette (with a bewitching smile)—"Dear doctor, (looks about her, nodding to the other two) I saw from the hall window what looked like—a man—who was it?"

Dr. W. (severely)—"Probably Jeremiah, the gardener."

Juli.—"I think I will walk about the garden a little."

Dr. W.—"I refuse to allow it. I have most carefully considered your needs, and have decided that you shall spend this morning in learning some parts of Herbert Spencer's philosophical works. Here are the places marked."

Juli. (pleadingly)—"Ah, not just yet, dear doctor." (Long, tender look.)

Dr. W.—"Now—at once—here." (Places her on low stool front stage right centre. (Juli. takes book, and sits dreamily.)

(Enter Tony, right, with golf sticks. Slaps Juli. on back.)

Juli. (turning)—"Ah, Tony, was it you whistling this morning? I thought at first it was a m—"

Dr. W. (interrupting)—"Miss Juliette, you are not to mention the word 'man' again this morning."

Juli. (saucily)—"Dear *man!*"

Dr. W.—"Grr—! You need keeping in order, young woman!"

Tony.—"Doctor, I shall go mad if I am not allowed to do *something*. Let me go round the links this morning. Gad, you know, old fellow, it wont do. I can't let myself get soft this way."

(Dr. W. takes away the golf sticks and puts them at back.)

Mili.—"Your lack of refinement, Tony, is impossible, considering your lack of funds. You'll get no one that is any one to marry you, if you will be so outrée."

Tony.—Rot, Millie! Ye gods and little fishes, you're painted again."

Mili. (haughtily)—"If you suppose I want a nose freckled like yours, you are mistaken. One must keep one's complexion white somehow in this sun."

Eliz.—"Yet the flowers let the sun choose *their* colors. Surely we ought also to trust him. Let me see—the cat tail bids the negro be content; the sunflower leads the Chinaman to his golden

tint; the Indian sees the deep hue of the sweet-william and turns his red visage sunward. What can we daisies ask better than that he should edge our petals with pink?"

Tony.—"You're stung, Millie, you'll get no pink tips to your petals under all that whitewash."

Mili.—"I need—and will yet get—tips of another sort,—no matter how. And I assure you I need whitewashing."

Dr. W.—"Miss Tony, this chair has been prepared for you."

Tony.—"That—sofa! Me—on a lounging thing—never!" (Stamps her foot.)

Dr. W.—"You will do as I tell you, if you please, while you are in my establishment."

Tony (after pause)—"Right you are! That's only fair. You're the captain. Now then fellows! Dive and tackle low!" (Vaults into steamer chair.)

Dr. W. (sighing)—"You will please stay there now, and darn these stockings as neatly as you can." (Places them in her lap.)

Tony.—"The deuce! This is no cinch, I can't darn,—oh hang it, you're chaffing me." (Gives back basket.)

Juli.—"I don't know why you should make such a fuss, Tony. We are none of us doing what we like."

Eliz. (plaintively)—"Hardly."

Mili.—"Nor what we do well, I assure you." (Delicately dusts glove.)

Tony.—"True. Well, give me the darn things." (Laughs and rolls up her sleeves.)

Dr. W.—"Now we are settled. Now I can read my mail."

Tony (watching Eliz.)—"For the love of Mike, Liz, can't you aim straight?"

Dr. W. (turning her chair)—"Keep your eyes away from that target, Miss Antonia." (Returns to his mail.)

Tony (after a moment)—"Golly Millie, you

just broke the head off that one, never got the root at all. Pull harder."

Dr. W. (turning her front-face)—"*Will* you keep your eyes on your sewing, Miss Tony?"

Tony.—"You-bet-cher life I will, old boy, if Liz'll shoot straight, and Millie'll pull a bit harder."

Mili.—"I will Tony. Let me alone." (Dr. W. returns to his mail. Mili. takes "Elwell on Bridge" and a pack of cards out of her parasol, and lays out test hands on grass, while Dr. W. reads scraps aloud unconsciously.)

Dr. W.—"What's his name, now? (Reads.) 'Etheldred Ranisty.' Coming to-day—hm—and his case! (Juliette has pricked up her ears.) (Reads.) 'My symptoms are of an abstruse and complicated nature. My mind is a tremendous and insatiable minotaur, which I have nourished upon the souls of men and women. A philosophic stream of profound thought and psychic emotion was poured unceasingly into my soul. Yet I starved! Women, upon whose tremulous loving hearts I played, palled on my imagination. Men whose inmost secrets thrilled me for a time, as I drew them out by my hypnotic eye, at last ceased to awaken in me the same ghastly grandeur as of yore. I sought greater emotions and deeper thoughts, and for a while lost my inertia among the teeming city slums. But even that fails now to hold my interest, my own strange inner rumblings of volcanic power absorb me. My eyes are bent inward, and the doctors tell me that my reason totters—' Hm—hm—very interesting case! (Reads.) 'Philanthropic efforts—self-analysis become a mania—the world is full of tongues—' Seven page tongue Mr. Ranisty has!"

 (During the latter part of this discourse Eliz. also pays attention.
 Tony stretches herself. Mili. plays cards.)

Dr. W. (looking at Juli., who hastily buries herself in book)—"I fear I was reading aloud—" (Mili. throws her skirt over the cards.)

Juli. (abstractedly reading)—"It has been truly remarked that in order of precedence decoration precedes dress."—"The wearing of ear-rings, finger-rings, bracelets, the elaborate dressing of the hair, the still occasional use of paint—" (Glances at Mili.)

Dr. W. (looking over her shoulder)—"Those are not marked passages, Miss Juliette."

Juli.—"Ah—no? No, so they aren't. I am so sorry. (Reads.) 'The general problem which comprehends every special problem is—the right ruling of conduct in all directions under all circumstances.' 'The truth that the production of animal heat—' Oh I can't learn this. It's all about *the fattening of* CATTLE."

Eliz. (softly)—"In the feminine border where the proud gladiola (looks at Mili.) stands so stiffly, where the red rose (Juli.) has glowed so warmly, and the field daisy (Tony) has raised her saucy head, and where (modestly) the heliotrope has filled the air with poetic odors, a *tulip* is about to spring up, bold and manly." (Dr. W. has been running distractedly through the seven or eight sheets of the letter.)

Dr. W.—"Ah, a telegram! Let me see! (Reads.) 'Neurasthenia, too much big game shooting. Arrive twelve thirty,—Mark Stone.'— Brief and startling. Well, well, I must make arrangements." (Tony shows excitement. Exit Dr. W., left. Juliette drops book and springs up.)

Eliz.—"Two tulips!"

Juli.—"Two *men*, Elizabeth." (Catches Elizabeth round the waist and waltzes.)

Eliz.—"Oh, Juliette, let me go! Why must you whirl with the turning spheres because man, the tyrant, invades our garden?"

Mili. (contemptuously)—"Because Juliette is an unbalanced compass needle. She turns, not only to the north, but to all the other points."

Juli. (crossing to her and shaking her gently)—

"Well, don't *you* care that we are to have two men to play with?"

Mili. (rising)—"I see no reason for getting excited. Men, to my mind, are not toys, but bread and butter machines—"

Juli.—"You—bread and butter—"

Mili. (laughing)—"Well, clothes-and-jewels-machines then. And *these* men don't sound promising."

Tony. (to Eliz.)—"Do you suppose he's been in Africa or Asia? In the deserts do you think?"

Eliz. (dreamily)—"In the deserts of the hearts of men, dry, arid, parched,—seeking the green oasis of some kindred soul. I feel, I feel that I—"

Tony. (interrupting)—"Oh fudge! I mean Mark Stone. He must have had a bully time. Golly, I wish I was a man! But I'll make him tell me!"

Juli. (to Tony)—"You talk as if one could get things out of a man with a club."

Tony.—"Perhaps not with a club, but with a six shooter,—you bet!"

Juli.—"Not at all, my dear. The only way is to roll your eyes at them, and the sooner you learn it, the better for you." (Juli. looks languishingly into space.)

Tony. (imitating her)—"So?"

Juli. (indignantly)—"I never looked like that in my life. But any woman who wants to, can win any man."

Mili.—"It is such a waste of energy to quarrel, girls. The real root of the matter is that any woman can *come near* to winning any man;—*and fail.*"

Eliz.—"He comes—ah-h—"

(Enter Dr. W. with Ranisty, left.)
(Eliz. gazes at Ranisty. Juliette gives him one look, and then coyly buries herself in her book. Tony barely glances at him. Mili. eyes him carefully.)

Dr. W.—"Ladies, may I present our new inmate, Mr. Etheldred Ranisty." (In dumb show Dr. W. presents R., leading him across from one to the other, while Mili. and Eliz. speak.)

Mili.—"What a tie! I sha'nt even ante, let alone betting. He's not worth my while."

Eliz. (aside)—"Not tulip,—monkshood."

Dr. W.—"And Miss Milicent, Mr. Ranisty."

Mili. (haughtily)—"How do you do!" (Turns back to weeding. Juli. moves toward him, and is about to speak. Elizabeth rushes to Ranisty's side.)

Eliz.—"You also have learned that the deeper claims of the soul sap the bodily strength. How bitter it is to find the trunk too weak to bear the branches. And yet we would not leaf less abundantly."

Ranisty.—"No, ah—hm—no."

Dr. W. (leading R. away in front of Juli. and Eliz.)—"I must leave you for a short time to the care of these ladies, Mr. Ranisty, while I consider your case, and ahem—er—" (Eliz. follows R. to stage left front.)

Mili.—"Run the first rough survey of his road back to nature." (Exit Dr. W. left, chuckling. Mili. returns to her cards, Juli. stands by her trying to interest her in the *man*. She tries to interest Juli. in the *game*.)

Ranisty (to Eliz.)—"Our excellent, but too practical, friend the doctor here seems persuaded that all profound analysis leads to morbidity, and eventually to insanity. I contended that analysis conducted on a broad enough basis and in a wide field had nothing in common with mere narrow self-analysis."

Eliz.—"Surely he admitted that."

Ranisty.—"He denied me the wide field, insisted that my only *real* interest was *myself*. That may be so. But no man, having the herculean mind and titanic nature of which I know myself to be possessed, can be called narrow, if he dwells upon the possibilities of such a self."

Tony. (staring at him)—"Mad, by gosh!"

Eliz.—"Tell me more. All my roots are drinking in and absorbing your words."

Ranisty. — "I find that women are *always* held spellbound when I even *begin* to unveil my personality. I do not blame them. To me it is an absorbing study." (Sees Tony feeling her biceps.) "What is she doing?"

Eliz. (carelessly)—"Oh, her muscles are very hard. You recall Browning's immortal words,—
'I am made up of an intensest life,
Of a most clear idea of consciousness
Of self, distinct from all its qualities,
From all affections, passions, feelings, powers;—' "

Ranisty.—"Ah—hm—yes,—but *I* like to do the talking."

Eliz. (not hearing him)—
" 'But linked in me to self-supremacy,
Existing as a centre of all things—' "

Ranisty—"Yes,—ah—yes. (To Tony.) How did your muscles become hard?"

Tony. (casually)—"Golf."

Juli.—"You don't play, I am sure, Mr. Ranisty."

Ranisty.—"Play! *I play*, when we have, so far as is yet proved, only one earthly life in which to watch *ourselves* develop!"

Eliz.—"It is so wonderful to find some one—"

Juli. (interrupting)—"Would you care to tell me what has brought you here? To me the fact that you are a man and the only one here, is so deeply interesting. I should like to know why. Do talk to me about it." (Eliz. crosses to Mili. who laughs contemptuously at her troubles.)

Ranisty.—"Certainly, I only ask to have an opportunity to discourse to an attentive and discriminating woman. What else have I demanded of life?" (Eyes on Tony.)

Eliz. (to Mili.)—"Juliette is so indelicate in her ways! But what congeniality can there be

between the rose and the grave, sad aconite! (Going out.) Whereas with the heliotrope—" (Exit right.)

Juli.—"You were saying—?"

Ranisty.—"What is golf?"

Juli.—"A hoydenish game, Mr. Ranisty."

Mili.—"Requiring less skill than the gentle game of man-snatching." (Juli. gives her an angry look.)

Juli.—"Mr. Ranisty, when you found your footsteps turned toward the House of Rest, had you no premonition of what you would find here?"

Ranisty (gazing at Tony)—"None. I thought I had plumbed all the depths of consciousness. But *this* is something new,—new and untried."

Juli. (tenderly)—"Yes? But not unwanted or unwelcome—?"

Ranisty (eyes on Tony, who is balancing a feather on her nose)—"I hardly know as yet. If I could only speak—"

Juli.—"Alone! Yes. I think I will go for a little walk in the gooseberry garden." (Gives him a long look, and exit slowly left, turning once more to look at him.)

Mili.—"Her methods are feline! And she has no style."

Ranisty (going eagerly to Tony's chair)— "Miss Antonia, pray explain to me your theories of bodily perfection. I do not feel that I fully comprehend the hardening of muscles." (Enter Dr. W. and goes to Mili., who hides her cards under cushions on garden bench.)

Tony.—"I should smile!"

Ranisty.—"You will not refuse to enlighten my ignorance! I am always seeking deeper chords in my own being, and you stir a new one."

Tony.—"Oh rot. Do shut up!"

(In dumb show R. goes on talking, Tony snubbing him.)

Dr. W.—"Poor fellow—mind very much affected. What do *you* think of him?"

Mili.—"Frightfully dingy!"

Dr. W.—"Well, you see, he has been living in the slums for some time. Philanthropy!"

Mili.—"It's really no longer smart—that sort of thing. The fad for it's going out."

Dr. W.—"But he has so much money (Mili. starts) that he can't get rid of his whole income, even by injudicious charity, let alone modern philanthropy."

Mili. (guardedly)—"How much do you suppose he has, poor fellow?"

Dr. W.—"Oh, several millions—" (Going.)

Mili. (with a cry of joy)—"Several million!"

Dr. W. (suspiciously, returning)—"P e r h a p s I should not have mentioned it."

Mili. (on guard again)—"Oh, I sha'nt speak of it, of course. (Exit Wheat-I-Eat.) Several million! (Flings her trowel from her and crosses to Ranisty who is just leaving Tony in despair.) Mr.  Ranisty, has Tony been boring you with her extreme ideas? You must'nt let her. Do tell me something about town. I've been away so long."

Ranisty (glancing at Tony)—"I had rather *you* would tell me something about my fellow-patients."

Mili.—"I shall be charmed to. Juliette—you know of course *who* she is—is taking a long rest here while some poor playwright tries to dramatize Bernard Shaw's plays.—I wish him joy of it!"

Ranisty.—"And Miss——"

Mili.—"Elizabeth is a half-cooked philosopher,—a sort of jam that didn't jell. We still expect to see her take more solid form."

Ranisty.—"Quite so. But Miss——"

Mili.—"Myself? Oh, I'm a diamond that's

been too much cut and polished, if such a thing is possible. They're hoping I'll get back into the rough."

Ranisty.—"But Miss Antonia——"

Mili. (impatiently)—"Oh, Tony! Tony is a tomboy. When she leaves here, no doubt she will be the essence of femininity."

Ranisty—"I have had large experience of women of the most complicated kinds, and Miss Antonia's simplicity seems to me——"

Mili. (impatiently)—"Oh, simplicity! She's very bad form, and her clothes are dowdy."

Ranisty. — "Clothes? What superficiality! Yet one of our modern philosophers says—'Since that day when Adam and Eve discovered their lamentable *lack* of clothing, the subject of dress has been of perennial interest to the human race,'— only however as an introduction to the statement that 'the body is the dress of the soul,' and the further profound observation that 'the soul secretes the body as the crustacean secretes its shell.'"

Mili.—"How disgusting!" (Aside.) "Pshaw, that was one of my impulsive mistakes in policy,— I must be fascinating and witty. (Aloud) "To us Americans dress is a philosophy of itself."

Ranisty.—"Ah, you are an American? Do you care for England as a place of residence?"

Mili.—"A poor exchange, don't you think—the land of the free, for the land of the fee? (Aside) Witty but unwise! (Aloud) But the breeding and cultivation and luxury of England—"

(Juliette has entered left, and breaks in.)

Juli. (reproachfully)—"*I* went to the gooseberry garden."

Ranisty.—"Oh yes, did you?"

Juli.—"You should have seen how lovely—"

Mili.—"Really, Juliette, you must not interrupt us. Mr. Ranisty and I are having a brilliant conversation."

Juli.—"You think it's taking to be witty, I

suppose. But you don't seem to have succeeded very well." (Ranisty is gazing absorbed at Tony.) (Enter Elizabeth and goes to Ranisty.)

Eliz.—"My monkshood!"

Ranisty (surprised)—"I beg your pardon!"

Eliz.—"You need not. Hardly any one ever understands me. But I hoped *you* would."

Ranisty.—"I assure you I don't."

Juli.—"Elizabeth, I hear you dreamed about the Man of Wrath last night again. I should think you would avoid the sex in future."

Mili.—"Really, Juliette, considering that your experience with that Tanner brute has taught you nothing, how can you expect—"

Ranisty (escaping to Tony.)—"Good heavens, I used to crave admiration, adulation, but now—!"

Tony.—"Pick up that spool, will you? Oh, get a move on!"

Ranisty (meekly)— "Certainly, if you will give me one."

Tony.—"Give you? Ye gods—the man's half-witted."

Ranisty.—"I have certainly discovered a void in my cerebellum."

Tony.—"Will you go! I'm sick of the sight of you,—and it's my role to be frank—"

Ranisty.—"To call a spade a spade—"

Tony.—"No, to call it a damn shovel. *Will* you go!!" (Exit Ranisty with one appealing glance.)

Mili.—"Que diable, Tony, you grow worse and worse!"

Juli.—"If *I* were a man, Tony, I should shake you."

Tony.—"You couldn't, Juli., you're not strong enough." (Pushes her away, hurting J.'s arm.)

Eliz.—"To think that when one eager soul

bridges the empty skies, he—perverse planet—should reach out toward other suns! (Weeps.) (During this Mili. has remonstrated with Tony, who sticks out her tongue.)

Mili.—"Really, Tony, your under-breeding is—is—"

Tony.—"Say it—'dingy!' (throws stockings and work bag on the ground and leaps up) Golly, but I'm bored! Mark Stone ought to be arriving! (Runs off, turns as she goes to say) Cheese it! Here's old Wheat-I-Eat!"

(Enter Dr. W. right, wheeling a wheelbarrow piled high with packages of wheat-I-eat and four tin pails. Tony slaps him on the back and vanishes.)

Dr. W. (looking after her, and leaving the wheelbarrow)—"Goodness gracious, well, well! All of you idle, all excited, and arguing,—I may say, quarrelling. Miss Elizabeth, you will go into the gymnasium at once and do dumb bell exercises for an hour till lunch."

Eliz.—"Oh, I beg of you!" (resists, but exit left.)

Dr. W.—"Miss Juliette you will go to the Home for Aged and Infirm *Females* and read to the inmates till lunch."

Juli.—"Oh, not now."

Dr. W.—"Immediately. (Exit Juli. right.) As to you, Miss Milicent, you will go and milk the cows and feed the chickens at once."

Mili.—"I?"

Dr. W.—"Go." (Exit Mili. right.)

Dr. W. (going to his place of entrance, and wheeling wheelbarrow across to extreme left front, then setting pails around on ground)—"Nothing like food in the open air! Let me see, Miss Milicent's pail,—so, so, so—(sniffing last pail) Wheat-I-Eat breakfast food, well cooked and allowed to cool." (Exit right as Tony and Stone enter left.)

(Stone, hung with guns and adorned with a pith helmet stalks in silently. Tony is talking as she comes in.)

Tony.—"Were you in Africa? Have you been in Uganda? Have you shot lions,—tigers? Do tell me! I'm crazy about sport. I say, where have you been, anyhow." (Stone is laying down gun cases.)

Stone.—"Central Asia."

Tony.—"Peter! Were there elephants? Have you been in the forbidden city? Did they try to assassinate you?"

Stone.—"Yes."

Tony.—"How? For the love of Mike, tell a fellow, wont you?" (Juliette has entered at back left of stage and watches, Mili. enters right back of stage and watches Juli.)

Stone.—"Dark night,—small bare room,—saw shadow on white wall,—jumped twenty feet aside, —knife missed me."

Tony.—"And what became of the man?"

Stone.—"Dead." (Stands with arms folded.)

Tony.—"How? I want to hear all about it. How did you do it?"

Stone.—"Choked him."

Tony (despairingly)—"Don't be such a clam! I say you know, it's not decent not to tell what you've done."

Stone.—"But it's Anglo Saxon."

Juli. (moves forward and catches her dress purposely on the target.) "Oh-h my dress! Oh, please help me. (Stone stoically unhitches dress,

—Tony grinds her teeth and stands glaring at Juli.) Ah, thank you. How strong your hands are! Are you Mr. Stone? The Doctor told us you were coming."

Tony.—"Where did you drop from, Juli.? Get out! Do!!"

Juli.—"Dear Tony, how mending does affect your temper! Mr. Stone, wouldn't you like to come for a walk in the gooseberry garden?"

Stone.—"No." (Makes for exit right, Mili. hides.)

Tony. (pursuing)—"Say, Mark, old fellow, don't go. Come and have a game of tennis, wont you?" (Exit.)

Juli. (following leisurely)—"*This* seems to me more possible than the other. How badly Tony does handle him! *I* must just try—" (Exit.)

Mili. (coming forward)—"Ha! Juliette cuts out! She prefers Mr. Stone. So much the better for you, my dear. I am utterly unscrupulous. *Tony* wont look at Ranisty. Remains Elizabeth to deal with. (Takes bottle of poison out of parasol and examines pails.) "No,—Juliette's, Tony's,—ah, here is Elizabeth's. 'Rough on Rats.' I wonder how much I need. 'Tasteless,—a teaspoonful will kill the healthiest rat.' Elizabeth is not very healthy, but then she is not a rat. (Dinner bell rings,—Mili. hastily pours.) I'll pour in so much. (The other three women seen entering—Mili. crosses to extreme right, concealing bottle.) Probably more than enough. I wish I were sure!"

(Tony, Juli. and Eliz. go to their pails and begin to eat, Elizabeth sitting on the ground.)

Tony.—"Same old Wheat-I-Eat breakfast food, same old sugar and cream! Isn't it beastly!"

Mili. (darkly)—"It might be worse!"

(Stone enters left and stands at back gazing at Elizabeth. She rises clasping her throat and staggers forward.)

Tony.—"Oh rats! It couldn't." (Mili. starts.)

Juli.—"Where do you suppose Mr. Stone went to?"

Tony (viciously)—"Anywhere to dodge you, Juli. It's disgusting the way you chase the man."

Juli.—"My dear Tony, you yourself—"
(Elizabeth shrieks and falls in a dead faint. Stone catches her with a cry.)

Stone (having laid Elizabeth in Tony's chair)—"My love! My life!"

Tony. (running off right)—"Where's the Doctor? We need a stretcher."

Mili. (to Stone)—"This seems so sudden! Have you ever seen her before?"

Stone.—"No. What need! I'm no modern." (He and Juli. fan Elizabeth.)

Juli.—"Here they come."
(Enter Dr. W., Tony and Ranisty with stretcher.)

Dr. W. (feeling Elizabeth's pulse)—"Dear, dear, how extraordinary! Now, Stone, just lift her—"

Stone.—"I'll take her head—" (They lay Eliz. on stretcher and carry her out.)

Mili. (to Juli.)—The telegraphic man is getting quite loquacious."

Juli.—"I wonder if she did it on purpose to get him."

Tony.—"Fudge! She'd never have the nerve. She looks as if she was done for!"

Mili. (aside, following Eliz., etc.)—"I must be quite sure that she is out of my path." (Exit.)

Ranisty.—"Miss Antonia," (follows her to extreme left of stage front, Juli. follows them).

Tony.—"Is that old philosophy again? Wouldn't that jar you!"

Juli.—"Mr. Ranisty—"

Mr. Ranisty (to Tony)—"It cannot be that

an unbridgeable gulf divides us, Miss Antonia. Could we but find the gossamer threads of sympathy that must bind together our, seemingly so distant, shores, we might weave a firm tissue of common thought and interest between us."

Tony.—"All I understand of that jaw seems to make me out a spider. None o' your lip, young man."

Ranisty.—"Indeed, you mistook my meaning."

Juli.—"Please don't upset yourself Mr. Ranisty. Tony's manners are quite impossible. Let me ask you how you feel about those social problems that you have so struggled to solve. Does not the whole answer to them seem to you to lie in that peculiar magnetism, that intangible, wonderful bond, that we call love?"

Ranisty (inattentive)—"Oh no,—er—yes—certainly. I beg your pardon, Miss Tony, that was merely a metaphor about gossamer threads."

Tony.—"A metaphor! Your grandmother! Is that Dutch for sass?

Juli.—"Mr. Ranisty, is it possible that you do not appreciate—"

Ranisty (not even hearing her)—"Miss Tony —Tony—I beg of you to let me speak. I understand that I cannot pretend to the vast and varied vocabulary that you so deftly wield,—but—"

Tony.—"Talk plain English then, and if you know how, lick your lips and look pleasant."

Juli.—"Etheldred,—ah, I beg your pardon. What a traitor one's tongue can be—" (He pays no attention to her.)

Tony.—"I say, Juli., three's a crowd. Clear out!"

Juli.—"Really, Tony—" (Eliz. has entered on Stone's arm, and sits languidly on garden bench extreme right.)

Ranisty (to Juli.)—"You understand, I feel sure, that when two souls—"

Tony.—"If you mention souls, I'll stop my ears."

Ranisty (hastily)—"I—I—not for worlds would I allude to them again. It was merely by way of elucidation to others—"

(Juli. turns away disgusted to the other two. Stone is standing with folded arms, gazing adoringly at Elizabeth. Ranisty in dumb show goes on talking to Tony, who is whittling a stick and half snubs, half allows it.)

Juli.—"I hope you're better, Elizabeth. I think, Mr. Stone, you said something this morning—"

Stone (to Eliz.)—"Darling!"

Eliz.—"I don't understand you. You are so abrupt."

Stone (to Juli, who is about to sit down)—"Leave us alone, please."

Juli.—"Leave! Well I never—! (moves half way down stage, looks at one couple then at the other. Shrugs shoulders.) The only other man in sight's the Doctor, and I've no more time to waste." (Exit hastily right.)

Eliz.—"I gather no meaning from these monosyllabic exclamations."

Stone.—"I love you. Be mine."

Eliz.—"I really cannot see that we have much in common. Tell me what are the winds that blow through your soul."

(Stone goes on talking and making love to Eliz.)

Tony.—"Gosh, how you do talk."

Ranisty.—"I would do more than talk, if you would permit me."

Tony.—"I don't believe you can do anything else! Gas-bag!" (Ranisty tries to take her hand, she slaps him.)

Ranisty.—"Women have *always* adored me. I do not understand why you alone—"

Tony.—"Oh, just for joy!"

(Ranisty goes on making love.)

Eliz.—"Your soul can be but a seedling, hardly above ground. I wonder if you even have one. I think not. And to me a soulless man would be an impossible husband, a leafless tree, a flowerless plant. I would have you—let me see—a tiger-lily, whereas now you are a mere unspiritual potato plant."

Stone.—"Wait then. I've hunted everything else. I'll hunt a soul now. I'm an Anglo Saxon, I cannot fail."

(On the other side, Ranisty has tried again to take Tony's hand as he speaks.) (Dr. W. and Juliette enter slowly right and wander to front right near to Eliz. and Stone, Juli. hanging on his arm and making eyes at him.)

Ranisty.—"I will prove to you that I am a man!"

Tony (snatching up Eliz.'s pistol and aiming it at him)—"Prove it then. (He flinches.) Pshaw, fraid-cat! It's not even a real fire arm, go and learn something."

Ranisty.—"I will. For your sake I will go and shoot things in the wildest forests. Only in the end, sweet affinity of my spirit—"

Tony. — "Yes, if you'll quit talking!" (Ranisty tries to take her in his arms. Tony puts the target between herself and Ranisty and dodges him. Stone stands with folded arms gazing down at Eliz., who is shyly gathering a flower which she puts in his buttonhole. Mili. enters and takes in the whole scene, gets out her big bottle of poison from parasol.)

Tony.—"Fooled again, Reddy!"

Juli.—"Wheaty-eaty, dearest, you know it has always been *you* in my inmost heart."

Stone (to Eliz.)—"Darling—"
Mili.—"Foiled! (Drinks poison.) I have failed! (Flings away bottle.) Death rather than a dingy future!" (Staggers to front left centre, shrieks and falls. Dr. W. catches Mili. and lays her down, others gather round in horror. Dr. W. empties the wheelbarrow, he and Stone lift Mili. into it and wheel her off, the others follow, snatching up their dinner pails.)

EXEUNT OMNES.

Printed by Libri Plureos GmbH in Hamburg,
Germany